Mark Ashton was the first person outside Oxford ____
out for wisdom when I was appointed as a very green
young Rector of St Ebbe's. Reading this wonderful book
has reminded me how many of my priorities have been
significantly shaped by his example, from sitting under his
feet when he first arrived at the Round Church, and by his
teaching. All who read it will be challenged, as I was, to
sharpen their focus and raise their standards for the great
benefit of the church and the glory of God.

VAUGHAN ROBERTS
Rector of St Ebbe's, Oxford
and Director of the Proclamation Trust

Many of us selfishly felt that Mark Ashton was called to
glory too soon. But, although no longer in this world, he
still speaks and we ought to be very grateful to Christian
Focus for republishing 'Christ and His People' that first
appeared in the opening chapter of *Persistently Preaching
Christ*. Several others have written about their priorities
as pastors of local congregation, but I am convinced that
Mark's principles are outstanding. I would want every
pastor and trainee pastor to read this book, and then for
all elders and indeed his whole congregation to read it and
hold their pastor to these priorities. In short, it is a 'must
buy'. Must read as must put into practice book. Thank
you Christian Focus for republishing it, and thank you
Mark.

JONATHAN FLETCHER
Recently retired Minister, Emmanuel Church,
Wimbledon, London

Christ and His People

Eight convictions about
the local church

MARK ASHTON

Copyright © Mark Ashton 2016

paperback ISBN 978-1-78191-829-6
epub ISBN 978-1-78191-830-2
Mobi ISBN 978-1-78191-831-9

First published in 2012 as a chapter in *Persistently Preaching Christ*
(ISBN 978-1-84550-982-8)
First published as a standalone book 2016
by
Christian Focus Publications Ltd,
Geanies House, Fearn, Ross-shire
IV20 1TW, Scotland
www.christianfocus.com

Cover design by Pete Barnsley, Creative Hoot

Printed by Nørhaven, Denmark

CONTENTS

Writing in the final months of his life before his death from cancer, Mark Ashton passes on his convictions about the priorities for the local church.[1]

---

1.   In a short booklet, *On My Way to Heaven*, Mark Ashton describes his own experience of facing imminent death from inoperable cancer. Real confidence, he explains, is found in the resurrection of Jesus Christ – an event which, even though it happened 2,000 years ago, has profound implications for us today. The booklet is full of hope and ideal to give away to others..

FOREWORD

Many readers of the eight short chapters of this fine meditation by Mark Ashton will instantly think of the much longer book by Mark Dever, *9 Marks of a Healthy Church*. Although these two books are quite different – what you are holding in your hand is the pastoral reflection of a man who knew he had no more than a few months to live, while Mark Dever's book is a theological/pastoral treatise – what is striking is how much agreement there is between them. Yet both can be read with enjoyment and profit, for they make their appeals in fundamentally different ways.

*Christ and His People: Eight Convictions about the
Local Church* is a touchingly personal book, clearly
written with the people of his own charge in mind.
Mark Ashton tells many stories of his predecessor,
Mark Ruston, who served as vicar of the Church
of the Holy Sepulchre in Cambridge – a church
building always referred to as 'The Round' or 'The
Round Church', a usage which no one who has seen
it will think strange. Under Mark Ruston's ministry
the church grew steadily, reaching out into the
University. Mark Ashton succeeded Mark Ruston
in 1987, and after the congregation outgrew the
building, it moved to a refurbished church building
that was no longer being used, but which was much
larger. So here was the congregation of The Round
Church meeting in St Andrew the Great – almost
inevitably referred to colloquially as STAG. Here
the faithful ministry of Mark II, as some referred to
him, combined with the unceasing hospitality and
cheerful witness of his wife Fiona, served generations
of students while reaching out steadily into the city
– a wonderful mixture of town and gown. Mark
Ashton has chosen to articulate his eight convictions
about the local church by summarising, in each case,
his principal point, and then fleshing it out with
stories of the ministry of The Round / STAG across
more than half a century.

Everyone who knew the man will never forget the
first letter he circulated to his congregation shortly
after he was told that he had contracted terminal

gallbladder cancer. He calmly told his flock that he had been given a great privilege: he knew, more or less, when he was going to die (though he lived about a year longer than the doctors had initially predicted), and thus he could prepare for his death – a privilege denied those who have no idea when they will die. His attitude reminded me of the old Puritan hope that it would be given to them to 'die well'.

This is the man who has left us this short book. Each chapter has a mix of aphorisms, wise pastoral judgments, and that most uncommon gift, common sense. Under 'Bible', we are told that '[t]he Word of God does the work of God by the Spirit of God in the people of God.' The primacy of the local church leads Mark to talk about the dangers of becoming too big and the importance of church planting. While stressing the importance of public meetings, he provides some culture-specific judgments about length of meetings and length of sermons. I must say in passing that he was a master of the 20-25 minute sermon. Dick Lucas has been known to argue that there are some 20-minute preachers, some 30-min preachers, some 40-minute preachers, and so on. One of the problems is that most of us think our number of minutes is higher than most of our hearers do. Several times I heard Mark at large conferences preaching for 45 minutes, and he was faithful to the text, but vaguely uncomfortable. But in the 25-minute range, no one was clearer, more succinct, more telling, in a time allotment that some preachers use just to get their motors warmed up. His chapter on 'Focus' – encouraging the local church to do a few biblically-mandated things very well, rather than trying to do everything – is sheer gold. As one of his curates put it, 'We are not trying to prevent people divorcing: we are trying to get people to heaven' – knowing full well that such gospel-centred ministry not only prepares people for the new heaven and the new earth, it also transforms people so they live differently here and now, thus preserving many marriages. Mark kept a plaque in his study with the words of William Perkins on it. Perkins, of course, was one of the connecting links between the continental reformation and England. He preached in the STAG building toward the end of the sixteenth century, so his words are especially *à propos*: 'Thou art a minister of the Word; mind thy business.'

Mark Ashton minded the business God gave him, and I am thankful beyond words that his pastoral wisdom shines forth in the pages of this little book. He, being dead, yet speaks, and we do well to listen.

D. A. Carson

Eight convictions about the local church

These eight convictions are not intended to be an exhaustive account of how a church should run, but they are distinctive characteristics of the ministry of this particular church, and I dare to think they are sufficiently normative (as well as normal) that they may be a help to others.

1. **Bible**: The word of God does the work of God through the Spirit of God in the people of God.

2. **Local Church**: The local church is the primary place where the Kingdom of Heaven impacts the kingdoms of this world.

3. **Expository Preaching**: Consecutive expository preaching by the pastor-teacher is the best normal diet of the local church.

4. **Meetings**: The meetings of the local church are for both edification and evangelism (with no sharp distinction between these).

5. **Ministers**: The ministers of the local church are all its members.

6. **Focus**: The local church should focus on doing a few things really well.

7. **Sacrifice**: The local church exists for the sake of others.

8. **Prayer**: Prayer lies at the heart of the local church.

1

BIBLE

The word of God does the work of God through the Spirit of God in the people of God

From the creation of the world ('And God said', Gen. 1:3) to the end of this present age ('with a loud command', 1 Thess. 4:16), God speaks his will into being. God the Son is called 'the Word' (John 1:1, 2). God the Father, God the Son, and God the Holy Spirit use the word of God to bring about all God's purposes. That word is living and active (Heb. 4:12). The Triune God creates and shapes his people by it. It is not the people who create the word. So, although the early Christian community wrote the New Testament documents, it was the word of the gospel that had brought that community into existence in the first place.

When Simon Peter acknowledged Jesus to be 'the Christ, the Son of the living God' on the road to Caesarea Philippi (Matt. 16:16, NIV 1984), Jesus called him the 'rock' on which he would build his church. When, six verses later, Peter denied that Jesus must suffer and die, Jesus called Peter 'Satan' (Matt. 16:23). So Peter was the 'rock' when he affirmed the gospel (that Jesus was the Son of God), but he became 'Satan' when he denied the gospel (that Jesus must suffer and die). It seems that the 'rock' was not Peter himself but the affirmation of the gospel on Peter's lips. The church is formed on and by the gospel, God's message of salvation. It is founded on Jesus Christ as preached by the apostles and prophets (Eph. 2:20).

The gospel is the message that we cannot save ourselves – neither by trying to be good nor by being religious – but that only God can save us, because he sent his son Jesus to die in our place. So through the death and resurrection of Jesus, God did for us what we could never do for ourselves: he paid the penalty for our sins. Now through his Spirit he can grant us eternal life, which is to have a relationship with him in Jesus' name (John 17:3). This is the greatest and best news our world has ever heard: that individual men and women, young and old, can be in their own relationship with the God who made the universe.

Mark Ruston preached faithfully about Jesus for three decades, and that word did the work of building

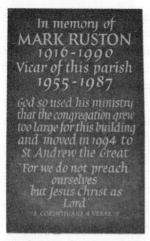

A plaque in the Round Church building celebrating Mark Ruston's thirty-two years of gospel ministry.[1]

up a congregation to the point where it could no longer fit in the Round Church building. The history of this particular congregation has followed that pattern for half a century. It is not a story of strategies, plans, and visions for future development. The regular teaching of the Bible has shaped the strategy through the shared leadership of the church. It is the preached word that has led the church forward. Human agency has been shaped and guided by the Spirit of God through the word of God preached weekly. Trying to respond obediently to God's word as it has been taught week by week has been the way the congregation has discovered what God plans for our future. Present obedience has been more important than blue-sky planning. One of the biggest changes that has occurred in the history of the Round Church was the move from the Holy Sepulchre (Round Church) building to the St Andrew the Great building in 1994. No individual can claim the credit for that. I went on record a few months earlier saying that I would resign if the church adopted a major

---

1.   Carved by Andrew Tanser BA ARBS of Guilden Morden, Herts

building project. But through regular Bible teaching God led the leadership of the church to the point where that decision was made by an overwhelming majority in the church council.

It is my belief that change has come about through the preaching, as God has spoken through his word week by week. I did not succeed Mark Ruston with any plans to change the Round Church. I came to try to preach as faithfully as my predecessor had preached. But change happened. The word caused it to happen. No doubt we do not always hear aright, nor do we always obey what we hear. But the word of God has the power both to bring the church into existence and to direct its life.

It has been my endeavour to allow God's word to do that and not to impose human systems upon it. Neither Mark Ruston nor I were systematic theologians. But both of us were committed to teaching the word of God as faithfully as possible, and then allowing it to do its work. Therefore, we have never sought greater clarity or more precision than there is in the word of God. For example, we baptise because the word of God tells us to do so. We do not try to indicate precisely what happens at the moment of baptism, nor at what age, nor in what manner it is appropriate for it to be administered, beyond the basic guidelines of Scripture: that baptism should be with water, in the name of the Trinity and in the context of faith. Similarly, we celebrate the Lord's Supper because we are commanded to do so in the Bible, and not because we understand precisely what it signifies.

Indeed, we pray because Scripture tells us to do so, not because we understand fully how prayer works.

This is not to say that we should not ponder these matters of Baptism, the Lord's Supper or prayer. But nor should we seek to achieve a clarity beyond Scripture. That way much disagreement lies, and no edification or evangelism occurs. We do not expect to get God's will exactly right. We expect the word of God to be constantly correcting us. God said through his prophet Isaiah: 'Whether you turn to the right or to the left, your ears will hear a voice behind you, saying, "This is the way; walk in it."' (Isa. 30:21, NIV 1984). It is a mistake to think of Christian discipleship as a straight arrow. It is more of a constant zigzag, as we veer first too much in one direction and then too much in the other – just as Simon Peter needed to be affirmed when he called Jesus, 'the Christ, the Son of the living God' and rebuked when he sought to deflect him from the Cross. Such is the nature of our human state. That means we need a word from God to correct us *every* day. This is true for churches as well as for individuals. Both need a constant touch on the rudder, correcting each effort we make to obey. God's word provides that.

The word of God doing the work of God will also mean that gospel work must always be done in a gospel way. There is never room for cutting corners, or selling people short, when it comes to the gospel. We have to seek to teach the whole counsel of God, however counter-cultural that may be, and however unpopular to contemporary ears.

The greatest single conviction about the local church that characterises the Round Church at St Andrew the Great is this: that the word of God does the work of God through the Spirit of God in the people of God.

2

LOCAL CHURCH

The local church is the primary place where the Kingdom of Heaven impacts the kingdoms of this world

To return to Matthew 16, Jesus told Peter that he would build his church on that rock of gospel affirmation on the lips of his disciples. He then made it clear that this church community would be an expression of divine power on earth, able to conquer evil: 'The gates of Hades will not overcome it' (Matt. 16:18). Indeed, the church would so incarnate the gospel message of God's saving love through Jesus Christ that Jesus went on to say, 'I will give you the keys of the kingdom of heaven; whatever you bind on earth will be bound in heaven, and whatever you loose on earth will be loosed in heaven' (Matt. 16:19, NIV 1984). What the gospel community does on earth reverberates in heaven. The rest of the New Testament is the story of small Christian communities being brought into existence by the gospel (the word of God) in different locations around the Mediterranean world (Acts 14:21-28; 15:41; 18:23; 1 Pet. 1:1-2, etc.).

The local church is not spoken of in the New Testament as a part of the universal church, but as the full local expression of the universal church in a particular place. It is 'the church of Jesus Christ at a particular place' rather than 'the little bit of the church of Jesus Christ at a particular place'. So, we need to view the local church in the light of God's calling – 'a chosen people, a royal priesthood, a holy nation, a people belonging to God, that you may declare the praises of him who called you out of darkness into his wonderful light' (1 Pet. 2:9, NIV 1984). Or, in the quotation attributed to G.K. Chesterton, the church is 'rushing through the ages as the winged thunderbolt of thought and everlasting enthusiasm; a thing without rival or resemblance, and still as new as it is old'. Therefore the honour of teaching a local church is enormous. Thomas Carlyle is said to have asked, 'Who, being called to be a preacher, would stoop to be a king?' I remember Giles Walter (curate at the Round Church 1986 to 1993) asking me at the Round Church door after the evening service one Sunday, 'Can you think of

'the honour of teaching a local church is enormous'

anything in the world we could have better spent our time doing these last twelve hours?' I could not.

The key characteristic of both Mark Ruston's ministry and mine is that we concentrated on the all-absorbing demand of running a local church, in the belief that this is a great task – greater than climbing the structural hierarchy of the Church of England, greater than getting involved in denominational politics, more significant than speaking at conferences, or travelling the world, or even writing books about the local church! Not all Christian leaders are called to this work; God sets people apart for all sorts of different roles within the body of Christ. But the best leader of a local church will be the person who is convinced that there is no higher calling in the world and that the New Testament role of pastor-teacher in the local congregation is *the* job above all others, and who is grateful to God every day for the privilege of serving in that way. Such are the men needed to lead our local churches.

Para-church organisations (like denominations and Christian campaigning groups) are necessary to help co-ordinate Christian work in a fallen world, which is full of misunderstanding and miscommunication even among Christians. But the size and the glamour which can accompany the work of such organisations should not distract from the top priority gospel work of the local church. The size and glamour of a very large local church have some of the same dangers. After moving from the Round

Church building to the St Andrew the Great building in 1994, the Round Church at St Andrew the Great took the decision not to try to go on growing in Cambridge city-centre, but rather to try to reproduce other medium-sized churches in the Cambridge area. We did not wish to become a mega-church, not just because this does not seem to be in line with New Testament practice, but more because it is not in line with New Testament principles, where God does his work through things that are weak in the eyes of the world (2 Cor. 4:7-12). Some of the consequences of this decision are described in Chapter 10.

It is because of this primacy of the local church that longevity in ministry is usually desirable. There may be a few men who are particularly gifted at leading a church through the early stages of growth, and then do best to pass the baton to someone else. But in general the best pastor-teacher will not be the one who is constantly wondering whether he should move on to new pastures or whether there is a better job on offer somewhere else. Patterns of church life which constantly move pastors from one church to another (as in the contemporary Methodist circuit) rarely build a local congregation over the years. It is characteristic of most of the strongest evangelical churches in the UK at the beginning of the twenty-first century that they have all enjoyed prolonged ministries by their main preachers. Mark Ruston served the Round Church for thirty-two years (and declined tempting offers to move elsewhere), and I have served the Round Church at St Andrew the

Great for twenty-two years (and would have loved to serve longer). As time passes in a preacher's ministry, it gets harder and harder to lead purely by innovation or human energy. But it is only with time that a minister gets to know and understand his congregation, and to be known and understood by them (even the changing congregation of a student church). Only by faithfully teaching the word of God will an individual's leadership stay fresh and revitalising over decades.

The second conviction that has shaped the ministry of the Round Church at St Andrew the Great is that the local fellowship of believers is at the very centre of God's purposes for the human race.

3

EXPOSITORY PREACHING

*Consecutive expository preaching by the
pastor-teacher is the best normal diet of the
local church*

A third conviction is that the healthiest and most
nourishing diet of the local church is the pastor-
teacher teaching the congregation the whole counsel
of God – in other words, taking them through
consecutive Bible passages week by week. If God is
the perfect communicator and the believer lives by
every word that comes out of his mouth (Matt. 4:4),
then there can be no better diet for a congregation.
Human lectionaries that 'butterfly' around Scripture,
flitting from one passage to another, will never
feed a congregation adequately. Too many local

churches, while paying lip service to the authority and sufficiency of God's word, insert the filter of the minister's own thinking and taste between the congregation and God's word when deciding on the church preaching programme. So the congregation only gets to hear from those parts of the Bible which the minister likes or thinks appropriate for his congregation.

Clearly there is a role for sanctified common sense. The wise teacher has to ponder, search out and set in order many things (Eccles. 12:9). So a planned preaching series is not inappropriate, but it must be shaped by the conviction that God is the perfect communicator and knows better than any human leader how to feed his flock. In the last resort, the word will do God's work. God does not need human agency. But he delights to use human speakers, when they are faithful to his word.

Mark Ruston habitually booked up the speakers whom the Cambridge Inter-Collegiate Christian Union (CICCU) had invited to give their Saturday night 'Bible Readings', in order to secure the ministry of the best Bible teachers in the country on a regular basis during term-time for the congregation. It was standard practice for a visiting speaker to speak for the CICCU on the Saturday night in the Cambridge Union Society building (or the large Lensfield Road Chemistry Lecture Theatre), to stay overnight with Mark Ruston in 37 Jesus Lane, to speak on the Sunday morning at the service in the Round Church, and to speak again on the Sunday evening for the CICCU's evangelistic sermon, often in Holy Trinity Church or Great St Mary's. A great many students of those days (including me) can testify to the superb grounding in Christian doctrine that such weekends provided. Having said this, my conviction was that I led St Andrew the Great most effectively by preaching regularly myself.

In practice, if a preacher is to be a true servant of God's word, he will have to give the best part of his days to studying the Bible for himself at his desk. It will mean the pain of hard and disciplined preparation, and prayer for God's help to apply the message of the passage into the realities of the society and individual lives of the hearers. The best sermons are those that have cost the preacher most, which means there needs to be an existential engagement with the word of God by the preacher through the week if the congregation is to be adequately fed on a Sunday. It will mean that from time to time the preacher needs to apologise to his congregation – perhaps because he has not worked as hard at the text as he should have done, or because he now realises that he got a previous passage wrong. He will not duck out of the harder and more challenging parts of the Bible. Of the two small Old Testament prophets concerned with the city of Nineveh, how often do we hear a series of sermons on Jonah and how rarely on Nahum? Personally, I found that preaching on the Song of Songs, Lamentations and the second half of Daniel (because they had been avoided in the preaching programme of the church for many years) proved to be a great blessing to me and, I think, to the congregation.

There is an important caveat to be made at this point: sequential exposition should be the staple diet of the local congregation, but it is not always the best way to handle the teaching programme of a youth camp or the equivalent. That may well be an appropriate place for systematic teaching where the key elements of the gospel of Christ can be taught in the limited time available. In that way the listener can grasp something of the whole plan of God in a short compass. Our minds are as weak and as sinful as the rest of our beings. And they need assistance in absorbing truth. So, the teaching programme for the youth group in a local church, or other group programmes, will not always be best served only by sequential exposition. There is an important place for 'systematic theology', which helps the human mind to comprehend and retain God's truth.

So, in general, expository preaching should be the staple diet for the local church. In his little book *The Priority of Preaching*, Christopher Ash (curate 1993 to 1997) makes the astute point that preaching is culturally neutral: 'Every culture knows what it is to sit and listen to an authoritative human being speak. That is not culturally specific. You do not

'expository preaching should be the staple diet for the local church'

need to be literate to do that. You do not need to be educated to do that. You do not need to be fluent or competent in debate to do that. Every human being can do that and that is what preaching is.'[1] He goes on, 'An interactive Bible study is not culturally-neutral. To sit around drinking coffee with a book open, reading and talking about that book in a way that forces me to keep looking at the book and finding my place and showing a high level of mental agility, functional literacy, spoken coherence and fluency, that is something only some of the human race are comfortable doing.'[2] The group Bible study, which we so value, has only been possible since the invention of the printing press, while preaching (one man addressing a group of people from God's word) has been the staple diet of the people of God from the time of the book of Deuteronomy right through to the twenty-first century. Regular expository preaching remains the staple diet for the healthy church.

Many church leaders agonise over how they can move a congregation from one condition to a better state. The answer is by preaching. Not by springing ideas, however biblical they may be, on the church council, but by feeding the flock with the word of God regularly, so that God's word pastors, leads, directs and changes both individuals and the whole body. It will move them step by step closer to his will. Such progress may not be apparent in the

---

1.   Ash, Christopher, *The Priority of Preaching*, Christian Focus Publications, 2009.
2.   ibid., pp. 27–28.

short term but, in the long term, faithful weekly exposition will move a congregation a long way; and through the Spirit it will create genuine change of heart and attitude in the congregation in a way that mere human leadership – however vital and inspired – can never do.

The third conviction about the local church is that its normal diet should be the sequential exposition of Scripture.

4

MEETINGS

The meetings of the local church are for

edification and evangelism together

(with no sharp distinction between these)

Most twenty-first century Christian believers assume that the Bible teaches us to meet together regularly in order to *worship* God. But the New Testament actually teaches that the whole life of the believer is worship (Rom. 12). As Christians we meet together, not specifically for worship, but so that we may encourage one another – in particular, to persevere in the faith and 'toward love and good deeds' (Heb. 10:23-25). Because all of life is to be a bowing down to God, our meetings ought to be characterised by corporate worship (bowing down together). But it is not as if we begin to worship when we meet and stop worshipping when we leave the meeting, any more than we start breathing when we arrive and stop breathing when we leave.

'Worship' is the concept by which we relate the whole of life to God. Whatever we do with our physical bodies is how we worship God (Rom. 12:1-2). So there is no part of life that has not become spiritual for the believer. The secular/sacred divide is removed by worship. So gatherings of Christians are not the special context for worship. And by using the term as if they were, we may reinstate an un-Biblical secular/sacred divide.

Those gatherings are for encouragement, edification (building each other up in our faith) and evangelism (see 1 Cor. 14). There is no sharp distinction to be drawn between edification and evangelism at Christian meetings. This is another distinction we love to make, thinking that a church service must *either* be aimed at building up Christians in their faith *or* at introducing non-Christians to the faith. But it is a distinction that the New Testament does not make. There, people are evangelised by being taught the truth, and they are pastored by being taught the truth. So edification and evangelism are both achieved by the meeting together of God's people humbly and attentively under his word. A meeting where we think the Bible passage speaks mainly to Christians ought still to contain the gospel of Jesus so that a visiting non-Christian will be evangelised. And a meeting *'our meetings must be designed to bring all human beings... to encounter the living God'*

(such as a Guest Service) aimed especially at non-Christians will bless and benefit the Christian, who also needs to be evangelised regularly.

Non-Christians frequently walk through the door of a church building. Every time they do, we must take them seriously. Church services should always be planned partly with the non-Christian visitor in mind. At one level this means introducing and leading the meeting clearly so that the newcomer is not embarrassed (when everybody around him or her seems to know what to do and he or she has not been told!). It also means that in preaching we try hard to show awareness that there will be interested non-Christians present. The inevitable interruptions that occur in the services of a city-centre church (buskers on the pavements, ambulance sirens racing past, roadwork drills) are welcome reminders of where we are and what our purpose is. Our meetings are set at the heart of the chaos that is modern life, which is not to say that there should not be moments of peace and quiet for reflection, but rather that church services must always take their context seriously. If we believe God's word will do his work, our meetings must allow that to happen. They must be designed to bring all human beings (whatever their spiritual state) to encounter the living God. The normal Sunday services of a local church can be its most effective evangelistic tool. But that means that every part of those services will have to be carefully planned with this in mind. A formal liturgy (if that is being used) must be controlled by this theological conviction: that the meetings of the local church are for edification and evangelism, as God's word does his work among his people by his Spirit.

Mark Ruston modelled his Sunday morning 'student service' at the Round Church on the type of independent school chapel service or fairly traditional Anglican morning service with which many of the undergraduates of the 1960s would have been familiar. This was not in order to appeal only to Christian students, or to just a particular social class of student. It was to pitch the service where it would have the widest familiarity among the undergraduate population of the time. A student could attend the service at the Round without any sense of encountering something unusual or strange. That allowed him or her to come under the sound of the gospel without having to deal with other unnecessary obstacles. It meant the word could do its work with a minimum of cultural interference.

The cultural and religious background has since changed beyond recognition. In the twenty-first century there is no equivalent model for our services, but we still seek to uphold the same principle of allowing the word to do the work without cultural hindrances. Therefore, we reckon that a service of about an hour's length is the appropriate duration in our particular (and in many ways unusual) culture. That allows Christian members of the congregation to invite their non-Christian friends with complete confidence that the service will end pretty well exactly an hour after it has begun. The young families particularly appreciate consistent control of the length of services, for the sake of their children, and any other families they may wish to invite. Christian congregation members might well prefer a longer service, but they need to be constantly reminded that church services are not for them alone.

This may mean restricting the usual length of the sermon for cultural reasons. It is a mistake to think that preaching is necessarily better for being longer. Most preachers preach less well for being allowed to preach as long as they like. A church that values preaching will endeavour to bring the best out of its preachers, and providing them with time guidelines is one way to do that. In Cambridge we have the privilege of hearing many great visiting preachers. It is easy to spot those who are not getting regular critical feedback on their sermons and are ill-disciplined about timing. John Stott became our model for always preaching exactly to the time that was suggested.

In order to avoid unnecessary barriers, we need to remove any possible cause of embarrassment from a service. We need to keep asking, 'Will doing this in this way in the service make someone feel uncomfortable?' And nothing has greater potential for embarrassment than music. Community singing is not a common activity in our culture now. Moreover there is a huge diversity of musical taste. It will not be possible to pick songs which please the taste of everyone present. So we have to select a position at some approximate cultural mid-way point for the sort of congregation attending the church service (and, at the Round Church at St Andrew the Great, the age demographic would be below thirty years old), and then try to do what we do with our music as best we can. Even though an item in a service may not suit my taste, the better it is done the less uncomfortable I will feel about it.

The pursuit of excellence communicates to the visitor that we are in earnest. The world will think us weak and unimpressive, but we need to show them that we think it matters and we are doing our best. There should be nothing shoddy about the way we do things. There should be no doubt of the seriousness of what we are about, nor of its accessibility. The outsider may not agree with the Christian faith, but he or she must be able to see that it matters a very great deal to us, and that we are communicating about it in terms that are intelligible to him or to her. It will be strange for a non-Christian in the twenty-first century to attend a gathering in which a fairly large number of his or her contemporaries are giving serious attention to a religious text two thousand or more years old. But we want them to feel as comfortable as possible in starting to listen closely to that text for themselves. It is helpful in every service to let the non-Christians present know that they are expected and welcome. A courteous and unembarrassing 'opt-out' or excuse not to join in with inappropriate parts of the service (like a Creed or a devotional song) can be given by saying something like, 'Not all of us will be able to say or sing these words'; and we try to answer within the first few sentences of any sermon the question in the mind of any bored non-believer present: 'why should I go on listening to this preacher for one more minute?' We try never to assume that only Christians are present (except at the monthly mid-week prayer meetings). We do not want the non-Christian to feel like an interloper, eavesdropping on a meeting of an esoteric sect, but rather to be reassured that it is all right to be present as a welcome guest who has not yet decided about Jesus Christ for himself or herself.

Because we are serious about what we are doing in our services, we can never take lightly the words we sing. Voltaire once said: 'If a thing is too silly to be said, it can always be sung', and we know the truth of that in the lyrics of some Christian songs. There are many popular contemporary Christian songs which we find we are unable to sing at the Round Church at St Andrew the Great simply because the words are unhelpful or doctrinally wrong. There are other songs where we have suggested changes in the lyrics to the author, and occasionally we have received their blessing to make that change. There is no doubt that congregation members remember the words they sing. It can be one of the most helpful ways of memorising Scripture. But singing is a dangerously powerful tool, and we need to be constantly alert as to whether it is building or undermining the faith of the congregation, and pointing the non-Christian faithfully to Christ.

Our fourth conviction is that the local church meets in order to hear God's word, which will edify the believer and evangelise the non-believer.

5

MINISTERS

The ministers of the local church are all its
converted members

The teaching of the Bible is not the leader's preserve. It is the task of the whole congregation. It is not confined to the pulpit. It actually goes on at every level of the church's life. While some individuals are paid to organise the church's life and to be free to teach the Bible publicly throughout the week, all Christians are ministers of the gospel. It is the privilege and responsibility of every Christian to teach others about God, and to live and work in the world for God. There are no more important tasks.

It will not help church members to think that the church is led by the people who take decisions on committees; so that the most important task a member can fulfil is to serve on one of those committees. 'How important am I compared with others?' is always an illegitimate question in the life of the local church. If the church is led by the word of God, then those who teach the word (in any form) are leading the church. Attending meetings, organising the church's life, or taking decisions are not at the top of a hierarchy of ministry. In fact there is no hierarchy of ministry and, if there were, such things would come low down the list.

As the Bible is taught in the congregation (with people then teaching each other), it will inevitably drive the individual members of that congregation out into the world to serve God in whatever he calls them to. All church members must be encouraged to think how they can serve God for themselves in the world.

There will be many different roles for them to play, and the rest of the congregation will not necessarily own those same roles or ministries. The Round Church at St Andrew the Great over the years has resisted pressure from individual members to adopt all the different ministries its members have been involved in. As a bachelor, Mark Ruston recognised that he had limited capability for children's, youth and family ministry. He focused on what he could do well (teach the Bible and minister to students) while allowing other congregation members to develop other aspects of the church's mission.

So we try to draw a notional boundary around what we concentrate our collective energy upon. It is the boundary of Bible teaching. We focus the church's resources on that, in the recognition that the Bible faithfully taught will then drive the church's members out into the world in all forms of Christian service and evangelism.

This is a generalisation in the life of the Round Church at St Andrew the Great, rather than a hard and fast rule. There are notable exceptions – like Bounce-A-Round, the large parents, carers and toddlers group which meets on a Wednesday. This is an example to the congregation of engagement with the world outside the church: it provides a service to the community, resourced by Christians, and is intended to provide a natural way for non-Christians to encounter Christ. In the same way, we have a small working group which addresses the issues of homelessness in central Cambridge on behalf of, and with the help of, the rest of the congregation.

But it is very easy for Christian social involvement to take on a life of its own, so that it can come to dominate the life of a local church, resulting in the church gradually losing its own gospel heart and gospel purpose. Only when a local church understands that its primary task is to teach the Bible faithfully to its members will those members be guarded against distracting and diluting tendencies in their world involvement. They must be involved in the world, but they must remain centred on the gospel. Only Bible teaching can achieve that.

This is not to say that within the local church we do things together but, in the wider *'the ministers of the local church are all its converted members'* world, work alone as individuals. The nature of the Christian life is corporate and we always do things together as Christians, if possible. The normal word for a Christian believer in the New Testament ('saint') comes sixty-one times in the plural out of its sixty-two occurrences (and even the sixty-second occurrence, Philippians 4:21, is in a plural sense!).[1] The strong cult of the individual, which has arisen in Western society since the Renaissance and which gives us such a strong concern for privacy and confidentiality, has little to do with the Christianity of the New Testament. There we are encouraged to invest heavily in one another's lives, to work together for God's kingdom on earth. And so we must. But this does not mean that every local church should adopt everything that each one of its members gets involved in. One fatal temptation for the local church is to take on too much. If we believe the word of God does the work of God, we can trust it to equip the people of God to do what God wants done in his world. The local church leadership must concentrate on the primary task

---

1. Based on the New International Version (1984). Other translations render the Greek as 'holy ones' or 'the Lord's people'.

of the local church – teaching the Bible faithfully to the congregation – while empowering and equipping the congregation members to be ministers of the gospel in many different spheres and ways.

So, in order to free the members to serve God as he calls them to, we have found it necessary to limit the activities of the Round Church at St Andrew the Great. Meetings are restricted to certain nights of the week so that church activities do not invade the entire lives of church members. (Committees meet on Mondays, Bible study groups on Wednesdays, aiming to leave other evenings free.) As a congregation we very rarely advertise other Christian causes, not because we do not approve of them, but to lower the pressure on each other's lives. Local churches can run on guilt; but just as grace, not merit, is the heart of our theology, so gratitude, not guilt, should be the heart of our ethics (our Christian behaviour). It is always a battle to restrain the 'internal temperature' of a church. It is always easier to start new meetings in church life than to stop ones that have passed their 'sell-by' date. If all the members of the congregation are its ministers, they must not have their lives so full of 'church' activity that they do not have the time or energy to be effective servants of the gospel in the world. It is the task of the paid church staff to free them up for that.

Our fifth conviction is that the ministers of the local church are all its converted members. They meet week by week to be taught the Bible to equip them for their many ministries.

6

FOCUS

The local church should focus on doing a few

things really well

We have already discussed the priority of Bible teaching and the danger of dissipating the church's energies by adopting too many programmes and ministries. Most local churches can do only a few things really well. To teach the Bible properly will require a lot of the church's resources to be dedicated to that end. But this principle of focus will have other consequences in the life of the church as well.

Being located in the centre of a city with a number of other churches meeting only a few metres away has meant that the Round Church at St Andrew the Great has been able to concentrate on faithful Bible teaching without coming under intolerable pressure to be all things to all people. Mark Ruston maintained a very clear direction for thirty-two years which meant that he passed a very united church on to me. If a church is like a bus (as John Wimber once remarked), displaying its intended destination clearly for all to see, then thirty-two years is a long enough time for the passengers to get absolutely clear that this is the bus they want to be on, rather than one which is going somewhere else. Many church leaders, in an attempt to please as many people as possible, have their churches displaying a confused message about their destination, which causes frustration and false expectations among the membership. So one result of a clear focus at the Round/St Andrew the Great has been a united congregation.

Mark Ruston also recognised his own limitations as a church leader and learnt to play to his strengths. With a background in independent schools and in school and college chaplaincy, he had a special gift for dealing with students one-to-one. He was an expert 'personal worker'. Such ministry is intensive. A lot of time and energy is poured into just a few people. Mark Ruston had carefully chosen students to lodge with him at 37 Jesus Lane because he knew the value of dealing in depth with a few in order to reach the many.

It is striking how narrowly Jesus focused his ministry. He concentrated on the Jews largely to the exclusion of Gentiles. He used parables to sift out from among his casual listeners those with a genuine interest (Mark 4:11). From his serious followers, he picked seventy to send out; but from within the seventy he had a prior commitment to twelve; and even within the twelve he chose three to accompany him at a number of key moments in his ministry: the raising of Jairus' daughter, the transfiguration, Gethsemane. Even within those three Jesus singled out Peter for special attention (and perhaps also 'the disciple whom Jesus loved', John, the author of the fourth Gospel). Undoubtedly, Jesus could have influenced more people – many more were eager to come within his orbit – but there was a clear focus to his ministry. He worked outwards from strength, building up one or two of a small inner group, and then the twelve, and, from that unlikely beginning, founding the church that has spread throughout the world. No single life has been as effective as his in impacting the whole human race.

'there was a clear focus to Jesus' ministry'

Mark Ruston showed the Round Church at St Andrew the Great the value of investing deeply in the lives of a few other people. 'Personal work' is a feature of the church's ministry. We try to provide the most faithful Bible teaching we can from the pulpit. We try to ensure that the Bible is at the heart of the programmes for the children, youth, students, young adults, home groups, internationals and senior members. We help members to set up prayer triplets, where three friends meet regularly to share needs and pray for one another. But we particularly encourage two Christians (often an older and a younger) to get together with an open Bible to discuss and apply God's word. All the church's staff members are expected to be a part of this. It is in such meetings that much of the most effective discipling of the church goes on. When two people are looking at the Bible it is much less easy to fall into the trap of applying its truths to others rather than myself; it is natural to ask questions if I cannot understand a passage; I can get to grips with God's word and, more importantly, it can get to grips with me. And I often form a profound and life-changing relationship with another person in the process.

Even within this focus on 'personal work', there needs to be a focus on the simple truths of the gospel. I was converted on 7 February 1968 when, after vociferous arguments with undergraduate friends, I was introduced by these friends to Jonathan Fletcher who, instead of answering all my arguments, sat me down and explained the gospel to me. He showed me that I needed to *Admit* that I was a sinner (Rom. 3:23; 6:23), that I needed to *Believe* that Jesus had died in my place to deal with my sin (John 3:16; Isa. 53:6); and I needed to *Come* to him (Rev. 3:20). Without that simple explanation and challenge to respond, I had found it impossible to get a handle on Christianity.

At the heart of all personal work lies a simple gospel explanation. It may sometimes be too early in the life of a particular person to go over the gospel in such simple terms, but it is never too late. The gospel lies at the very heart of the Christian life and we never grow out of it or go beyond it. Every step forward in our discipleship is always also a step back to the foot of the cross. 'Personal work' focuses above all else on those simple truths; and it is in the light of them that a huge range of other topics can be tackled when we meet one-to-one. Mark Ruston brought many students to Christ with such a simple focus.

The gospel calls us to change – the change of conversion if we are not yet Christian, and the change of sanctification (growing more like Jesus) if we are. But, individually, we find it very hard to change ourselves. We need the help of a community – exhorting, challenging, rebuking, encouraging one another – which is why the church must always be a change-enabling community. And the most effective way the community helps me to change is one-to-one. Only there can I find the security to acknowledge my particular weaknesses, failures and sins and, with the help of one other person, confront and conquer them.

So there has been over the years a focus on personal work in the Round Church at St Andrew the Great, encouraging the members to speak personally to their friends, both to share the gospel in evangelism and to study it in discipleship. Personal work is one of the scarcely seen ways that God's word does his work in his world. It is an example of the value of focusing ministry, not on what the world approves and applauds, but on what God intends and purposes.

After twenty years of ministry in Cambridge I approached my churchwardens to ask whether they would consider freeing me up for a wider role in the church at large, a bit like a 'Rector emeritus'. I felt that I had focused within Cambridge quite narrowly for two decades, and it might now be appropriate to play a rather different role, while the very strong staff team handled the day-to-day running of St Andrew the Great. The churchwardens, under John Anstead's leadership, asked for time without me present to ponder the question and then in effect replied, 'No'! It was a little more nuanced than that – the exact words of their memo were:

> *In principle, the wardens are in agreement that you should be able to do more work away from St Andrew the Great. However, we believe that God has called you to serve him as our main Bible teacher and leader of our congregation and that this should continue to be your principal area of service. We feel that this is vital, not only for the lay congregation, but also for our paid staff and those who are considering full-time Christian work. We would still expect to see you present and active, either preaching or leading, at the majority of services.* (Email from John Anstead to Mark Ashton, 6 June 2007).

After initial disappointment, I realised just how affirming such a reply was. The team of four churchwardens was absolutely clear that I was doing what God intended me to do, and I could not be more profitably engaged in the service of the kingdom anywhere else. So I withdrew my request.

That affirmed for me the value of focus in the local church – that the cost of doing the most important things of all as best we can will always entail neglecting other good and worthy things. We need to learn to distinguish what really matters from what matters, but matters less. One missionary used to have a plaque on his desk that read 'Planned Neglect' to remind himself of just this point. At Christopher Ash's suggestion, I had over my desk the words of the Puritan divine, William Perkins (who preached in the St Andrew the Great building at the end of the sixteenth century) – 'Thou art a minister of the Word; Mind thy Business!' (Christopher Ash named his golden retriever 'Perkins', which seemed less useful!). C.J. Davis (curate 1994 to 2000) once helpfully clarified the aim of the Marriage Preparation ministry at St Andrew the Great by saying, 'We are not trying to prevent people divorcing: we are trying to get people to heaven.' In other words, the team members were not pretending to be marriage counsellors or sex therapists; they were teaching the Bible to engaged couples as the surest way of guarding their future marriages. We needed to keep our eye on the ultimate goal in order to achieve the intermediate goal of healthy Christian marriages.

Focus in the local church will mean ignoring many of the things that the world expects us to do (the things that often bring the most glory and honour in the world's eyes) in order to channel our resources into the (often less glamorous) tasks God calls us to.

7

SACRIFICE

The local church exists for the sake of others

Archbishop William Temple perceptively remarked that 'The church is the only co-operative society in the world which exists for the benefit of its non-members.' Self-sacrifice is a hallmark of healthy church life.

The pattern established by Jesus himself (Phil. 2:4-11) is one of self-humbling. But it is not just humiliation for its own sake. Isaiah 53 teaches us that the pain of substitution is balanced by the blessing it brings to others: 'But he was pierced for our transgressions, he was crushed for our iniquities; the punishment that brought us peace was upon him, and by his wounds we are healed' (Isa. 53:5). 'Taking the pain so that others may get the blessing' is the biblical pattern for the individual Christian life and for the life of local churches.

Mark Ruston taught the adult congregation to serve the student community in the centre of Cambridge. 'Town' members of the congregation quickly learned that the church had a mission to undergraduate students which was costly and inconvenient. The Sunday morning family service would change its meeting time six times a year, as it was moved forward in term-time to make room for the later student service, and then reverted out-of-term to a more convenient, mid-morning time. Changing service times is thoroughly uncomfortable for families and non-student members of the congregation and, at every change, some forget and arrive embarrassingly early or embarrassingly late. No text book on *How to Grow a Successful Church* would ever advocate such a tactic. But there must be few more eloquent reminders to a congregation that they do not exist for their own convenience.

When I started as vicar of the Round Church in 1987, I was advised by an experienced leader of a large student church in another country to aim to wrap up the work of the university Christian Union in my first couple of years. Adults can minister to students much more effectively than students can minister to one another, and a student work resourced and staffed by a local church will, in human terms, 'outcompete' a student work run by students for students. But I followed the pattern I had inherited – that the Round Church served the student work of the Cambridge Inter-Collegiate Christian Union and did not try to dominate it, and that has remained our endeavour. God has delighted to use the weakness of student leadership to his own glory, as God always delights to use human weakness (1 Cor. 1).[1] Another senior church leader of a student church provided another, more pragmatic, rationale for supporting student leadership in student work: 'If the CICCU goes off the rails theologically,' he said, 'it can be back on again in a year or two. But if a local church goes the same way, it can take decades to restore it.' So if we allow student work to be dominated by local churches, the potential for harm is very great.

At the end of the 1980s, the Round Church Parochial Church Council, after various revisions, agreed a 'Vision Statement' which tried to encapsulate the church's conviction. One of its three main statements reads: 'A church committed to a specific mission: it is our special task to serve the university communities in which we are placed. There are two aspects to the work of our church ("town and gown"), but both depend on one another: by becoming a better "normal" church, we also become a better student church.'

All healthy churches need to have a mission for which they sacrifice themselves, and a focus for that mission in some 'target' group. This point was made powerfully by a local minister who wrote:

---

1.   Barclay, Oliver R., *Whatever happened to the Jesus Lane lot?* Inter-Varsity Press, 1977.

Do you want to know how to kill a
church? Fasten its members' attention
purely on internal matters. Get them
agitated about what hymnbook they
should sing from. Make them anxious
about charismatic enthusiasm in
their midst, or about the sins of the
ecumenical movement. Get them totally
absorbed in a new building programme,
or in fund-raising activities, or in
simply being nosey about one another's
problems. It does not really matter what
the issue is, so long as it has the effect
of drying up their outreach. Then stand
back and wait for spiritual gangrene to
set in and do its lethal work. Go back a
generation or two later and you will find
that church has become one of those nasty
cliques that are dominated by a handful
of inter-bred families who cannot give
up the habit of church-going. The church
will have been murdered. To be more
precise, it will have committed suicide.
If such a church remains orthodox, it is
a dead orthodoxy; if it retains a congregation, it is a lifeless congregation. As
often as not, of course, they do neither.
They simply disappear, leaving their
once busy churches to be turned into
factories or mosques.

A young family joined the Round Church early in my ministry and after a year the father complained to me that he had come to realise that any money he gave to the Round Church would not be spent on a youth worker to look after his two teenage children, but on student workers to care for the students. He announced that the family was leaving for another Cambridge church with better youth and children's provision. I felt deeply apologetic that we had not made that clear to the family from the outset. We are a church that sacrifices our own interests for the sake of a mission to students.

But this culture of self-sacrifice has been a constant spiritual tonic to the vitality of the congregation. Just as long-term consistency in the ministry has united the congregation over the decades, so an attitude of self-sacrifice has kept the congregation gospel-hearted. It has sieved out from the congregation those for whom church attendance is primarily a matter of meeting their own needs, and which is to be done at their own convenience. The final sentences of that vision statement read: 'We believe that God means us to grow, individually and as a church; that growth is change; and that change may be painful. We accept the pain of change gladly for the sake of bringing the gospel to our contemporaries'. Accepting the pain of change gladly is much easier to say than to do, but in the pain of change we have discovered so much of God's blessing.

Trevor Huddleston once wrote a book with a most striking title – *Naught for your Comfort* – which seems a very good motto for local church life. It has been

'the gospel is never about seeking our own comfort'

wisely said that spiritually healthy churches lurch from one financial crisis to another. That dictum has been a comfort to many church treasurers, and one long-term member of the congregation at the Round Church at St Andrew the Great said that, in his opinion, the only time when he had been aware that the church was slightly stagnant spiritually coincided with a time of no financial worry. The gospel is never about seeking our own comfort, and it always drives the local church out to do more for God in the world.

After the completion of the rebuilding work on St Andrew the Great in 1994, the church leadership was not minded to expand the building's capacity in order to grow the church in that way any further. Instead we were moved by the Bible teaching to a conviction that we should seek to plant or graft a part of the congregation into other local church situations where the ministry was weaker. Consequently in 1997 Christopher and Carolyn Ash took forty adults and children to All Saints, Little Shelford (a village five miles to the south); then, in 2004, Steve and Beth Midgley took over 100 adults and children to Christ Church (a mile to the north east); and in 2008 Frank and Katherine Price took a similar number to St Matthew's (a mile to the east).

Each of these church plant leaders first joined the staff team at St Andrew the Great with the encouragement to preach so well that in a few years a good number of the congregation would happily leave St Andrew the Great with them to reinforce the life of another church. Fundamental to that model of church-planting is not just that it is a gifted Bible teacher or just a group of congregation members, but the two together: a Bible teacher with a group who want to be taught the Bible by that teacher.

When preparing for one of these church plants, any and all members of the congregation have been encouraged to sign up for it. There has been no selection process by the church staff. No-one has been ordered to go or forbidden to go. There has always been a period of prayer and preparation; particularly as such Church Growth Initiatives are peculiarly hazardous and problematic within Anglican structures even with the support of the Diocesan Bishop. Then, when the moment has come, the 'umbilical cord' has been cut at once – all financial giving transferred and everyone encouraged to make a clean break from the parent congregation. Each of the church leaders involved has been faced with a sink-or-swim situation; but, in view of the very tough first two years which Christopher and Carolyn Ash weathered in Little Shelford, we have since always tried to ensure that there was one other full-time staff member to support the church leader. All three of the men who have done this showed immense patience and supernatural wisdom and discernment. Grafting one body of believers on to another is hugely problematic. It is greatly to their credit how well all three churches flourish.

So the Round Church at St Andrew the Great has tried to be characterised by a generosity to other Christian work. We only give away approximately ten percent of our financial income to support other Christian work at home and overseas (knowing that there are many churches which are more generous than that), but we have tried to conduct our church life in a self-sacrificial way – giving away about a third of our student members every year, giving away a much higher proportion of the normal church congregation on a regular basis in church plants, and glad to accept the pain of that for the sake of others. We are convinced that self-sacrifice is essential in the local church.

8

PRAYER

Prayer lies at the heart of the local church

A final conviction that has shaped the life of the Round Church at St Andrew the Great is that prayer must lie at the very heart of the local church.

Mark Ruston's quiet godliness spoke of someone who prayed a lot. In his teaching there was always a firm insistence on the 'Quiet Time' – that every Christian should try to find a time to be alone with God every day. On their wedding day Mark Ruston would give couples a copy of *Step by Step* by John Eddison to take away on their honeymoon with them, so that they started married life together with the Bible and prayer at its centre.[1]

Prayer and Bible reading have to go together. The way the Bible works in the life of a believer is a mystery. It is not simply an authoritative text like the Koran. Frequently it compares itself to food, so that the spiritual life of the believer is maintained by God's word ('Man does not live on bread alone, but on every word that comes from the mouth of God', Matt. 4:4, NIV 1984). That is a dynamic image, where the believer has a part to play (eating and digesting the word). We do that by reading *and* praying over the word of God. So prayer is vital to Bible reading. In Deuteronomy 29:29, Moses told the people of Israel: 'The secret things belong to the Lord our God, but the things revealed belong to us and to our children for ever, that we may follow all the words of this law'(NIV 1984). Scripture is not a complete revelation of everything a human being might want to know. There are secret things which belong to God. But it is a dynamic revelation, revealing what we need to know in order to live God's way on earth. It interacts with my life to teach me how to live. And that happens through reading *and* praying. Every day I need to hear that voice behind me saying: 'This is the way; walk in it' (Isa. 30:21), and I need to respond to it in prayerful obedience.

---

1.   John Eddison's *Step by Step* is a brilliant aid to a daily 'Quiet Time' with selected Bible verses, a short comment and a very brief prayer for each day of the year. It has recently been reprinted by Authentic, ISBN 978-1-85078-819-5.

Prayer is how we engage with God's word, and how it engages with us. It is the place where God's Spirit gets to grips with our spirits to bring us into line with his will: 'In the same way, the Spirit helps us in our weakness. We do not know what we ought to pray for, but the Spirit himself intercedes for us with groans that words cannot express. And he who searches our hearts knows the mind of the Spirit because the Spirit intercedes for the saints in accordance with God's will' (Rom. 8:26-27, NIV 1984). It is a mysterious and largely invisible process. It is how we participate in the eternal spiritual realm, how we walk by faith and not by sight (2 Cor. 5:7). What God is doing is not easily visible to human eyes, so not all visible growth in a church will necessarily be his work. Our criterion for judging any strategy for the church must be its faithfulness to what he has said to us in the Bible, not whether it adds to our numbers.

> *'Prayer is the place where God's Spirit gets to grips with our spirits'*

Church growth methods and 'church leadership by statistical analysis' must be judged by this criterion. *We* do not grow the church or build the congregation, and, while we think we can, we probably get in the way of the only one who actually can.

But as it is Christ's intention to build his church, then we can pray that he will do so. And prayer is exactly the right attitude to the growth of the church. We cannot have a five-year plan for it, as though we can achieve it ourselves. It is not a human achievement. But we can pray for it, as God has made his will clear in the matter. And then we can expect it, as we expect answers to all our prayers, trusting God to act in his own way and in his own time, for our best interests. There is an important distinction between seeing church growth as something we achieve by 'getting things right' (by our own clear thinking and our hard work), and seeing church growth as something God grants as and when he chooses. When we are told that we should 'plan for growth', we can alter two letters and '*pray* for growth'. Our guideline for the future development of our churches should not be 'How can I increase the size of this church?' but 'How can I bring this church more into line with the will of God so that he can fulfil his purposes for her?' The answer is by attending to the Bible and by prayer.

Change in the local church always begins in the heart of its pastor. The pastor himself must be a person who is living under the reproving, correcting, exhorting word of God and responding to it in his prayer life. If the pastor does not change (and be seen to change in ways that are costly to him personally), he should not expect his church to change. For that he will need a vibrant prayer life. He will need a reserve of energy in order to pastor a changing church. Change is emotionally expensive for all concerned. So a church leader must take time to pray.

As well as the emphasis Mark Ruston always put on the 'Quiet Time' (for himself and for others), he also insisted on the importance of the church prayer meeting. A biblical church will always be a praying church. But finding an appropriate pattern for the corporate prayer life of a local church is a tricky business. Few things engender guilt as easily as our lack of prayer. 'Does this church pray enough?' is an entirely unhelpful question in the life of a local church (along with, 'Does this church care enough?'). The answer must always be 'no'! The prayer life of a church cannot be judged by mere quantity and it is never helped by guilt.

The recent pattern at St Andrew the Great has been to cancel all the Bible study groups on the first Wednesday of each month and assemble all who can come for a monthly Church Prayer Meeting. It has become a key meeting in the life of the church (if not *the* key meeting). It is the one gathering at which we make the assumption that everyone present is a believer – although even then we apologise publicly that we are making that assumption for the sake of any outsiders present. We start with a song, a prayer of confession and a Bible exposition; and then we break into smaller groups (of six to eight) for prayer, interspersed with slots of information to fuel our praying, and songs. It lasts an hour and a half. There never seems to be anything very special about the format of the meeting. But it is undoubtedly the very heartbeat of the church.

One subsidiary but important function of the Prayer Meeting is disseminating information and sharing, because it informs the prayer life of the church for the rest of the month, along with the monthly Church

'The monthly Church Prayer Meeting...is undoutedly the very heartbeat of the church'

Prayer Diary – the latter is a key discipling tool in the life of the congregation, as it teaches us and encourages us to pray. A church council member once said, 'If you miss the Church Prayer Meeting, you miss the news about what is going on in the life of the congregation.' It is the central hub, the heart of the church. The attendance and the atmosphere at the Church Prayer Meeting seem to provide an accurate barometer for the spiritual health of the congregation (in so far as such things can ever be accurately discerned by human beings). It is the group to which the church staff and churchwardens and church council first bring new ideas, suggestions or developments so that they are first prayed over by the church before they are decided upon.

I became more and more aware during my ministry how much I owed to the prayers of the church. I found the Round Church at St Andrew the Great a wonderfully easy church to lead, partly because of the unity within the church and the gospel-heartedness of the church which I inherited from Mark Ruston, and partly because Mark Ruston taught the church to pray – privately and together. Although the particular individuals changed over the years, the culture of the church had become deeply biblical and prayerful. That is a wonderful heritage.

Also available from
Christian Focus Publications

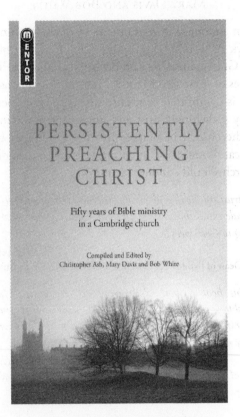

PERSISTENTLY PREACHING CHRIST

Fifty years of Bible ministry
in a Cambridge church

Compiled and Edited by
Christopher Ash, Mary Davis and Bob White

ISBN 978-1-84550-982-8

Persistently Preaching Christ

CHRISTOPHER ASH,
MARY DAVIS AND BOB WHITE

Gain a glimpse into ministries of Mark Ruston and Mark Ashton at The Round Church at St Andrew the Great church in Cambridge. Through the ministries of these two Marks, this local church was and still is committed to ministering to people, persistently preaching Christ and immersing the ministry of the church in prayer. This book provides theological thought and an example as to how any local church should conduct its ministry.

I trust this book will go some way towards helping us all understand the way the local church can be such a blessing to God's people.

Phillip Jensen
Dean of Sydney at St Andrew's Cathedral, Sydney, Australia

This book is both challenging and inspiring. Mark Ashton's eight convictions at the start and the emphasis throughout on the centrality and power of God's word are vitally important for all churches in any setting.

Vaughan Roberts
Rector of St Ebbe's, Oxford and Director of Proclamation Trust

CHRISTOPHER ASH

PROCLAMATION
TRUST MEDIA

THE PRIORITY
OF PREACHING

ISBN 978-1-84550-464-9

The Priority of Preaching

CHRISTOPHER ASH

"This little book is written for ordinary ministers who preach regularly to ordinary people in ordinary places... Most of us preach in gatherings that are smaller than we would wish and tougher than we might have hoped when we entered pastoral ministry... There is a voice on our shoulders who whispers as we prepare, and then as we preach, 'Is it really worth it?" – From *The Introduction*

Christopher Ash tell us that it is worth it. More than that, he sets out a charter for preaching that draws from the very roots of the Old Testament – showing us that nothing in the world is more worthwhile – for preaching is God's strategy to rebuild a broken world.

All in all I found this short book to be as helpful as anything that I've read in a long while on expository preaching. I commend it warmly to all.

Alistair Begg
Senior Pastor, Parkside Church, Chagrin Falls, Ohio

Christopher Ash is an ordained minister in the Anglican Church and Director of the Cornhill Training Course, a one-year course designed to provide Bible-handling and practical ministry skills to those exploring their future role in Christian work.

WHAT CHRISTIANS BELIEVE

JONATHAN GOULD

ISBN 978-1-84550-922-4

What Christians Believe

JONATHAN GOULD

What exactly is it that Christians believe? Whether you are a Christian looking for a refresher course on the essentials, or an interested enquirer, this book is for you.

Clearly and crisply explaining the core beliefs of the Christian faith, and interacting with the kinds of questions on our minds, many areas of confusion are clarified, and many questions answered by this wonderfully helpful book.

What I really admired about this book was that it not only clearly and relevantly lays out the Christian faith, it also then predicts the questions that may well arise in the reader's mind and gives a compelling response to those queries.

Rico Tice
Author, *Christianity Explored* &
Associate Minister, All Souls Church, Langham Place, London

With unapologetic pastoral clarity, Gould reminds Christians that Christianity is not about religious sensibilities added on to an otherwise worldly life, but about radically God-centered truth that completely reorganizes our lives for his glory. The result of these two concerns is that this is a book for anyone, believer or non-believer, who not only wants to know what Christians believe, but why that belief matters.

Michael Lawrence
Senior Pastor, Hinson Baptist Church, Portland, Oregon

Jonathan Gould serves as the minister of St John's, Downshire Hill, Hampstead.

EQUIPPED
TO SERVE

RICHARD BEWES

ISBN 978-1-78191-286-7

Equipped to Serve

Richard Bewes

Richard Bewes was born in a missionary family on the slope of Mount Kenya, attained a degree from Ridley Hall Theological College, Cambridge, and worked in Christian ministry until his retirement in 2004. His ministry in south-east England led to his post as the rector of All Souls Church in London for 21 years. What makes a Christian worker? What does it mean to give your life to Christian work? Richard Bewes' *Equipped to Serve*, is an answer that was built from a lifetime of ministry.

Through it all, the heart of a shepherd is modelled, explained and gently pressed upon us.

Michael Reeves
President, Union School of Theology, Bridgend, Wales

Richard Bewes has produced another treasure-a masterpiece of practical Christianity... A special gift.

Timothy George
Founding Dean of Beeson Divinity School,
Samford University, Birmingham, Alabama

Richard Bewes is the author of several beloved books of faith including T*alking About Prayer, 150 Pocket Thoughts*, and *The Goodnight Book*. Bewes was the rector of All Souls Church in the centre of London from 1983 until his retirement in 2004. In 2005 he was awarded an OBE for his services to the Church of England.

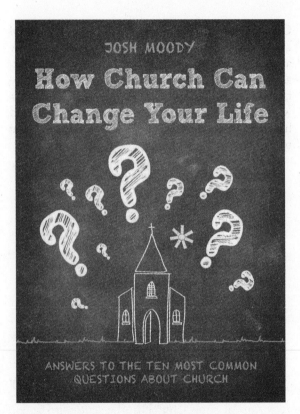

JOSH MOODY

How Church Can Change Your Life

ANSWERS TO THE TEN MOST COMMON
QUESTIONS ABOUT CHURCH

ISBN 978-1-78191-611-7

How Church Can Change Your Life
Josh Moody

Google books on church, there will be no shortage of choice! Some will be helpful, others less so. So why another book on church? Josh Moody, is, in fact, asking a very different question: why should I go to church at all? Filled with practical advice, this book will help you answer questions you maybe should have known the answer to and other questions you never knew to ask!

... a powerful and needed reminder of the central role the local church should play in the life of every Christian.
R. Albert Mohler
President, The Southern Baptist Theological Seminary,
Louisville, Kentucky

This book answers questions about the church that your friends are asking!... Read this book and be encouraged by his answers, and then pass it along to a friend who has considered church attendance to be optional.
Erwin Lutzer
Senior Pastor, Moody Church, Chicago, Illinois

This book is just brilliant!
Steve Levy
Pastor, Mount Pleasant Baptist Church, Swansea, Wales

Josh Moody is Senior Pastor of College Church in Wheaton, Illinois. His books include *Burning Hearts*, *Journey to Joy*, *No Other Gospel*, and *The God-Centered Life*. For more, visit www.GodCenteredLife.org.